Hands

MOYA CANNON was born in Dunfanaghy, County Donegal in 1956 and now lives in Galway. She studied history and politics at University College, Dublin and international relations at Corpus Christi College, Cambridge. Her first collection, *Oar*, won the inaugural Brendan Behan Award and, in 2001, she was the recipient of the Laurence O Shaughnessy Award (University of St. Thomas, Minnesota). A number of her poems have been set to music by Jane O Leary, Philip Martin and Ellen Cranitch, and she has worked with traditional Irish musicians, amongst them Kathleen Loughnane and Maighread and Tríona Ní Dhomhnaill, both in the context of performance and of translating Gaelic songs. Moya Cannon has edited *Poetry Ireland Review* and, in 2004, was elected to Aosdána, the Irish affiliation of creative artists. In 2011 she was the holder of the Heimbold Chair of Irish Studies at Villanova University, PA.

Also by Moya Cannon from Carcanet Press

Carrying the Songs

MOYA CANNON

Hands

For the Womens' Circle at
Brescia College.
Keep the flame,

Moya

CARCANET

Acknowledgements

I thank the editors of the following magazines in which some of the poems have previously appeared:

The Cork Review, Five Points, Nordic Irish Studies Journal, PN Review, Poetry International, Poetry Ireland Review, The Shop, Southword, The Stinging Fly, Temenos.

Sincere thanks are also due to the Centre Culturel Irlandais, Paris; the Virginia Centre for the Creative Arts, Amherst; and the Centre d'Arte i Natura de Farrera for their gracious hospitality during the writing of some of these poems.

First published in Great Britain in 2011 by
Carcanet Press Limited
Alliance House
Cross Street
Manchester M2 7AQ

www.carcanet.co.uk

A CIP catalogue record for this book is available from the British Library
ISBN 978 1 84777 142 1

The publisher acknowledges financial assistance from Arts Council England

Supported by
**ARTS COUNCIL
ENGLAND**

Typeset by XL Publishing Services, Tiverton
Printed and bound in England by SRP Ltd, Exeter

for John

Contents

Soundpost

'Its tone came from the soundpost –
it was made from a bird's bone.'
A musician tells of his friend's fiddle,
the one on which so many
well-shaped tunes
had been turned and played.

In French it is called *l'âme*,
the instrument's soul;
in Cremona, when the master-luthier
brought a supply of slow-growing timber
down from the high Alps,
to shape around his moulds,
it was called *l'anima* –

a round peg of wood,
positioned carefully inside the instrument,
almost under the bridge,
to hold apart belly and back,
to gather every vibration of the strings,
every lift and fall of the bower's wrist,
to carry all that is in us of flight,
through the woods of the instrument.

Reed-Making

for Cormac

Man is but a reed, the most feeble thing in nature, but he is a thinking reed.

Blaise Pascal

A strip of cane is whittled, gouged thin,
cut in two;
its concave sides are held together;
tapered ends bound, with waxed thread,
to a brass funnel,
then fitted into a chanter.

If one turns out well
and is played in
by a fine musician,
the lips of the reed
will come to vibrate in sympathy,
and all things will flow through them –
joy, grief, despair, and again, joy –
stories told in secret to a tree;
told to a reed;
carried back on a channel of air
into life's bright rooms.

What generates music?
Gouged, bound wood,
or wind, or breath,
playing on a tension between
what is bound and what is free –
a child blows on a grass blade held between two thumbs,
wind blows across the holes in a hollow steel gate,
and blood leaps in response –
a hare alerted in tall grass.

Driving back over the Blue Ridge,

you say that the leaves are late in turning.
Halfway up the wooded hill to our right
the sun has decanted itself
into a single maple tree.

There are days like that
which sing orange and red
in the forest of our ordinary green.

These are the days we hang our souls upon
as, high above them, the sun withdraws.

Openings

In my chest
a rusted metal door
is creaking open,
the door of a decompression chamber
cranked up on barnacled chains.

The rush of air hurts and hurts
as larks fly
in and out,
in and out
between my bended ribs.

Still Life

Much though we love best
those intersections of time and space
where we are love's playthings,
a sweet anonymity of flesh –
life's blessèd rhythm
loving itself through us,
two human bodies tuned
to the whirring stars –

this is almost nothing
without the small, quotidian gifts,
habitual caresses which hinder fears,
the grace of small services rendered –
two bowls of blueberries and yoghurt,
two cups of coffee,
two spoons,
laid out on a wooden table
in October sunlight.

All this green day

the sun has come down the valley and
turned the house-slates silver;
rain and hail have come down the valley;
small trees have curved down to the river
and the poplars have stood tall
and only a little bare at the top.

Here and there, in the green cloud of birch and hazel
above the hermitage of Santa Eulalia,
a wild cherry tree sings russet
and the mountain tops around us are furred with trees.

The bare peaks far to the east
have captured a first fall of snow;
the trees and mountains carry on
as though nature had not been conquered;
the grass deepens towards evening
and the little scalloped slates shine in the dusk.

Only the shadows

show us what light is —
the hard shadows of poplars
on the valley's green, warm floor;
broken shadow in the forefront of a Pissarro painting,
as a young woman washes dishes outside in sunlight;
shadows in our lives — sickness, loss, death.

Shadows
alert our vision
to the living light in clear-blooded trees,
dappled light on blue and white cotton,
washed light on stacked vessels.

October

In the very late morning,
the sun rolls up again
over a saddle in the high Pyrenees
and each roof in the village
is a slab of light.
The slated farmhouses
are grappled in tiers
onto the steep, south-facing
side of the valley, so that folded schist,
slate and marble insist
into the homes of humans upstairs
and into the homes of animals downstairs
and after heavy rain
little springs trickle in through the houses'
back rock-walls.

This morning,
each of those stone and slate houses,
warms up like a brick oven,
warms up like the small black cats
who cross the lanes of Farrera.
I sit at the east-facing kitchen window,
slicing fruit, drinking coffee and light
and sadness falls away from my shoulders.

Val de Luz

Light fills every
poplar and ash leaf
in the valley;
fills the leaves of the wild cherry and the birch
which have laboured for months
to turn light and water
into life and fruit
and which wait now
to be paid in gold.

Farrera Light

Why should the evening sun
which blasts light through the tops
of the slender yellow poplars in the valley
and of the red wild cherry trees on the hillside;
which lingers, a fillet of light in the dusk,
on the green ridge slanting down
to the hermitage of Santa Eulalia;
which shafts, a slightly opened blue fan,
onto range upon fretted range
of peaks to the east,
why should it shaft me too
with unaccountable joy?

No Good Reason

There is no good reason
why my heart should be so gladdened
by a green hillside which turns golden,
or by an echoing jangle of bells –
the mountain's many-hoofed glockenspiel –
or by the sight of the old, bow-legged shepherd
who, propped on his stick,
leans against his jeep and waits
for his son to bring down the flock.

Hands

for Eamonn and Kathleen

It was somewhere over the north-eastern coast of Brazil,
over Fortaleza, a city of which I know nothing,
except that it is full of people –
the life of each one a mystery
greater than the Amazon –
it was there, as the toy plane on the flight monitor
nudged over the equator
and veered east towards Marrakech,
that I started to think again of hands,
of how strange it is that our lives –
the life of the red-haired French girl to my left,
the life of the Argentinian boy to my right,
my life, and the lives of all the dozing passengers,
who are being carried fast in the dark
over the darkened Atlantic –
all of these lives are now being held
in the hands of the pilot,
in the consciousness of the pilot,
and I think of other hands which can hold our lives,
the hands of the surgeon
whom I will meet again when I return home,
the hands of the intelligent, black-haired nurse
who unwound the birth-cord from my neck,
the soft hands of my mother,
the hands of those others
who have loved me,
until it seems almost
as though this is what a human life is:
to be passed from hand to hand,
to be borne up, improbably, over an ocean.

Orchids

Today the ward is filling up with orchids.
Beyond the pink terraced houses and the January trees
the clouds break apart
to illuminate curtain after curtain of grey hail,
which batter in fast across the bay.

And tall orchids,
have arrived
in the cancer wards –
magnificent as crinolined beauties,
at the ball
before a battle.

Yesterday I was listening on the iPod

to Vivaldi's cello concerto –
so I did not hear the helicopter land
below in the hospital yard
or see them carrying in two stretchers.

Two hours earlier, a young woman,
half my age,
had fallen into the Atlantic with her son.
A long, long fall from the cliff top –
in a car crash the bonnet crumples so slowly –
I wonder if time slowed down for them
as they plummeted past layers of limestone,
layers of mudstone,
layers of the earth's time?

I wonder what terrors had flayed her,
whether they cried out to the fleeing earth,
whether she held him in her arms,
or by the hand,
and I wonder whether
some strong-winged angel
caught them both by the wrist
as they entered the tide at the cliff's foot,
whether there was light and music
to meet them –

and, if not, I wonder
whether Vivaldi's music can be
a bright bridge to nowhere;
or whether all of us can be
falling down time's long cliff,
each of us alone,
with all our fears in our arms.

Parisii

My father was a Paris cattle man.
Dante Alighieri, *Purgatorio*

The Parisii, who ferried travellers
across this shallow bend of the river,
with its two islands –
unmatched as the eyes
of a Picasso demoiselle –
lived on a worn trade route
which led north to wintry islands,
south to an empire,
and an inland sea.

They knew little of the glitter and tramp
of the Roman legions
that would soon bear down on their homes;
nothing of northern longboats
that would rip the river with their oars
or of tanks that would motor in over metalled roads;

they knew nothing of Attila
or of Charlemagne;
nothing of cathedrals, like tethered ships,
of the flourish of baroque courts
or the hour of the *sans-culottes*;
nothing of painted canvas,
jazz, or of heated café talk,

but, waiting, on the wooden quays,
to load silver or cloth,
or casting off in their tapered cots,
raw-knuckled, in February frost and fog
they must have known this –
dawn raddling the grey river
which separated two parts of Gaul.

Little Skellig

for Paul Cannon

It is not difficult to believe,
a little, in archangels here
as golden-headed gannets swoop
around our lurching boat.
They are poised
as spray-blown row upon row
of cherubim,
along the ledges
of a tooth of sandstone,
which, for centuries,
has been whitewashed with guano
until its galleries are luminous, clamorous
as New York or Singapore.

The boatman in his yellow coat
restarts the engine and twists for home.
Salt water sloshes across the deck
then one gannet plummets
and there is something
about the greed and grace
of that cruciform plunge
which shouts out
to our unfeathered bones.

Sea Urchins

These distant cousins of starfish
are dug into their hard honeycomb above the tideline.
Silently, they eat limestone
and the drifted shells of dead limpets.

They digest the rock in their soft innards,
to build coats of brown spines
and splendid, symmetrical carapaces
which the sea will occasionally
deliver to us intact –
sunbleached, rosy sea-lanterns.

The Fertile Rock

for Áine

In May evening light
an exhausted silver ocean collapses.
It has carried so much to this island,
blue rope and teak beams,
dolphin skulls and fish boxes,
and, once, a metal tank on wheels,
containing one cold passenger.

It rises and collapses at the rim
rises and collapses again –
a mile of white, salt lace
which races across the low limestone terraces,
invades every crack and crevice
in the brown, brine-bitten stone,
and sprays up over
a small grey plateau,
whose fissures brim
with sea pinks.

Lady Gregory at Cill Ghobnait

for Sheila O Donnellan

*It was St. Goban built that church…
she was a king's daughter
and could have married rich nobles…*
Lady Gregory's diary, May 1898

A tiny roofless room –
the rounded window-slit looks past
O Brien's castle to the rising sun –
outside, a granite quernstone
and two bishops' tombs,
a ruined beehive hut
and a tethered, grazing ass.

The patroness of beekeepers had fled
from her people, west across the sea from Clare,
unlike Augusta, who was rowed
across the Gregory Sound from Inishmore,
caught here five days in an October storm,
her son gone off to school,
her husband dead.

Years later, she returned in May, was handed down
from the steamer onto the currach's seat
and sat on the strand to watch three men
hold one end of a net on shore
as with the other end, three rowed out
to draw half a circle on the lit green sea.

And maybe one of the bantering men
was Peter Coneeley, who lost his father in a storm,
off the same strand, swept away with two more,
at the end of a human chain,
leaving this sloping field with its church
in the care of his widow and of his twelve-year-old son.

But on the day that Augusta walked west here,
and sketched the lintel and the leaning jambs,
Gobnait's bees hung, as today,
among bedstraw and whitethorn
and bright young grass.
Only five hundred miles to Euston
and to London's humming dinner tables, calling cards,
yet half of Europe's history lay between
Cill Ghobnait and St James's Park.

Sometimes two cultures are so opposed
through narratives of conquest and control,
that one sees nothing but the other's hackled back,
no shard of beauty, only cruelty and lack.
Sometimes, then, against the odds,
like a voyager alighting from a limestone boat,
someone is drawn to listen, then to act.
For myth and metamorphosis are allied,
shifting how we apprehend the world,
and imperium is dismantled in minds and hearts
or not at all.

Thirteen hundred years had passed
Since Gobnait left Cill Ghrá an Domhain
and travelled on from Inis Oirr,
told in a vision she would find her resurrection and her work
in the place where she came on nine white deer.
Somewhere between Gort workhouse and the House of Lords,
Augusta planted trees,
raised a stone at Raftery's grave,
turned her widow's loneliness to wealth and,
in good faith, did her best to find and mind
the best in both the worlds she spanned.

*Cill Ghrá an Domhain: Church of the Love of the World, the old name for Cill
Ghobnait.*

Nausts

There are emptinesses which hold

the leveret's form in spring grass;
the tern's hasty nest in the shore pebbles;
nausts in a silvery island inlet.

Boat-shaped absences,
they slope to seaward,
parallel as potato drills,
curved a little for access –

a mooring stone, fore and aft,
and a flat stone high up,
to guide the tarred bow
of a hooker, *púcan*, or punt

when the high tide lifted it
up and in, then ebbed,
leaving it tilted to one side,
in its shingly nest.

Eliza Murphy

What will survive of us is love.

Philip Larkin

Seventeen-month-old Eliza Murphy died
in eighteen twenty-seven
and was buried in April,
in a field south of a garden.

Perhaps spring gales prevented them
from rowing her body
across the short stretch of water
to blessed ground in Killeenaran.

We do not know what brought on her death –
fever, famine or whooping cough.
We do not know whether her hair was black,
or whether her eyes were brown.

We do not know who raised
the carved stone to her memory –
perhaps an older sister or brother, who, later,
sent money from America,

or whether, at low spring tide, she had ever
been carried across the sandbar to the mainland,
past regiments of squirting razor-fish
and sponges like staring moon-cabbages.

Neither can we be sure that she lived
in the row of cottages beyond the garden
or that she was born in one of the rooms
now brimming with sycamores.

We cannot be certain that she had learned
to balance on her feet before illness came
or was able to toddle about on the cobbles.
We cannot know her small store of words.

We know only that she sleeps
where the otter and the fox pad through the long grass
and that she died in April,
dearly beloved.

Crater

A high corner of the apple tree shakes
as a thrush pecks and pecks at one of the last apples.
The sun slants onto the thrush and the apple
which has a crater in it.

This is what apples are for,
to be turned into song.

The Magician's Tale

The magician I met in Leap Castle
told me that she had grown up
in a magicians' supplies shop in London.
Her father, a seventeen-year-old from Mayo,
his lungs eaten by tuberculosis,
had been nursed by her mother,
a young Londoner,
who, one Monday morning,
brought him a gift,
a book of magic tricks.

All his long months in the sanatorium he practised,
eventually honing tricks which only he could perform.
He could produce from the healed cavities of his chest
seventeen billiard balls,
and who knows how many handkerchiefs,
how many white, fluttering doves.

In the Underground Car Park

for Mary Armstrong

You noticed them first
as we walked back, lost in talk,
through that ill-lit bunker
glimmering with cars.

They drifted like dry pink snow,
blotting bumpers and bonnets,
catching in the iron patterning
of a round man-hole cover.

We drove around the pillars
of the dim underworld
and saw where they billowed
through the metal grilles,

then settled in a deep pink drift
on the grey concrete floor.
You ran and scooped handful
after handful into a summer hat.

The blossom was softer, finer
than anything we could remember –
like music drifted down to Hades
with a promise of cherries.

Brought to Book

Two long-haired young men yank at one another's beards;
two fat cats eyeball each other;
two mice tug at an altar-bread held between them,
as though wildness itself yearned for balance.

Oak galls were ground for brown ink;
the fur of the marten-cat
bound into a brush;
lapis, traded from Afghanistan,
crushed to blue powder;
gold tapped,
finer than fish-skin.

The deft, sharp-eyed young men,
in scriptoria at Kells,
Iona or Lindisfarne,
who bent over work so intricate,
only young eyes could see it
in all its ludic tangle,
may not have been unlike
Traveller boys I taught
who would rather have been charging
in a sulky down an East Galway road in March
or out in night-time fields, lamping rabbits,
than sitting, hunched over a desk,
ears cocked for the returning school bus.

When troubled, they too were calmed
by the rhythm of lighting up a page
with crimson and indigo pens;
their minds were soothed
by stories of terrible trials,
of survival and triumphant good,
involving lions, eagles, gods and men.

Loch

for Francis Harvey

To the side of a mountain gap,
light fills the scraped bowl
of high Loch Ochoige.
This lake is a secret to which
you can skid down, hazardously,
over a slope of quartzite scree,
or climb up from one of two valleys.
It is a minted silver coin;
a treasure dug out by glaciers;
it is a secret in which to swim,
its water cold, brown, a little bitter –
at each stroke you will tip a little water
over the lake's rough lip.

It gathers the mountains about it
and, as the sun moves around
the mountains are great shutters
like the shutters in Dutch paintings
which slant light onto a jug or a letter
or a lady's yellow cloak,
but here, light is slanted
onto an emptiness
which brims over,
which is replenished.

'We Are What We Eat.'

That's what she said,
'Every seven years
almost every cell in our body is replaced.'
I thought of her own art,
how faithfully she rendered
the miraculous lines, the miraculous lives,
of feather and bone –

and I remembered an oak rib,
honeycombed with shipworm,
given as a keepsake to another friend,
who had sailed from Dublin to the Faroes
in a wooden fishing hooker,
which was later rebuilt.

These boats are rebuilt, renamed,
until every plank and rib
has been replaced so often
that nothing remains
except the boat's original lines
and a piece of silver,
hidden under the mast.

Alma,

I woke up saying the word,
just as, a few mornings earlier, I had woken up
saying 'The Silk Road'.
Who conducts the music of our dreams?
leaving us with only one clear note – a word for 'soul'
or a name for the most sensuous, the most tortured, of early roads,
a name given at a distance, in hindsight,
by someone who had never travelled it –
not even one clear road either, but several,
a web of camel routes through thorn and sand and storm,
mule tracks over frozen mountain gaps
to where silk worms chewed on mulberry leaves,
spun from their bodies the strong filaments of dreams.

I thought

only love could do it,
give us moments so complete
there is nothing behind us or before –
only the timbre of that particular voice,
the brush of skin on that particular skin,
soul brushing against that other soul –
but, sometimes, light can do it too,
as it fills every fresh leaf on an April tree,
brightens one side of every limb and twig,
reveals how every one of them was pulled low
by last year's burden
and half the branches pruned and burnt,
how the tip of every down-turned branch, every one,
is upturned now, pink budding through the green –
like the painted, upturned fingers
of temple dancers.

Two Doors

There are two entrances to this house
the old priest told us this morning
as he turned, bright as a bird,
to the great oak door under the rose window.
Through one door the people come in,
through the other door the light comes in
and the people are in the light
and the light is in the people.

Few could have wished it otherwise
yet, in the cathedral's thousand years,
so much else has come in the lower door,
borne often by princes of church and state,
while, through the rose window,
through thick dust, through spiders' webs,
with their hoards of netted flies,
the light still enters, limpid, constant.

Coimbra, Portugal, 2010

Green Cities

for Brídín

Coming around a corner today at Rue Fouroy
The scent of newly clipped boxwood is
the scent of Dublin forty years ago,
the scent of summer cities –
a scatter of boxwood clippings on canvas.

Behind the double, upside-down u's
of the green iron stile
white butterflies,
and a man in worn corduroys.
His long-handled clippers click
the child-sized hedges into neat green blocks
opening onto a world of fountains spilling and spilling
their profligate freshness into the summer light.
Round flowerbeds,
musty with lupins, heavy with bees.

And the swings –
oak seats worn to satin,
with iron chains
creaking and creaking solemnly,
weight swinging us up,
in our short-sleeved frocks,
higher and higher,
into the fruiting chestnut trees.

Swans at Nimmo's Pier

They are angels at their morning ablutions
more industrious by far, more hygienic,
more conscientious, than mortals.

More than a hundred oil and rummage their feathers,
nibble themselves vigorously under stomachs and wingpits,
littering the shingle with white quills and breast down.

But in the middle of this white fury
some sleep on, long creamy necks coiled on their backs,
heads folded under their own glorious wings.

Most of these doze on the concrete slip
but a few sleep standing up,
meringues balanced on grey feet.

These dozers are Luciferian swans who,
heads hidden under unnibbled wings,
think darkly, 'I will not scrub.'

Or perhaps they are less resolute,
muttering in their angelic slumbers,
'O Lord, let my wings be well-oiled,
let me be louse free – but not just yet.'

The Washing

April light drenches the washing –
white sheets and pillowcases,
pink towels, blue jeans;
four more bean plants have shoved
their heads up through the horse manure;
green flames flicker
through the tarnished armour
of the apple tree's branches
and, from a breezy, budded twig,
a robin tells the cat that he, the robin,
owns the world.

Inside, on the windowsill,
the sun washes across a photo of my mother,
gentle and pretty in her furred degree gown.
My young father in another photo
poses by a pine tree with his fiddle.
The photos were taken,
long before they met
on two other light-drenched,
given days.

The Train

The railway embankment to our left
drives a green line through scree and grizzled heather.
A ghost track carries a ghost train
west from Letterkenny to Burtonport.
On one of the slatted wooden seats
sits a serious fourteen-year-old from Tyrone
with fine, straight, reddish hair.
The train huffs and clanks over our heads
across tall, cut-stone pylons
which flank the narrowest part of the road.

She is travelling to Irish college in Ranafast
in nineteen twenty-nine.
The narrow-gauge train steams along so slowly
that she can reach out
and pull leaves off the occasional, passing tree.
Her friend holds her hat out of the window
and swizzles and swizzles it around, absent-mindedly,
until it spins off and lands amid the scree.

My mother does not know that the railway line was built
by men who believed that the train was foreseen
in the prophecies of Colmcille
as a black pig snorting through the gap.
She cannot prophesy, so she does not know
that her father will be dead within three years,
or that she will meet her husband
and will spend her adult life
west of these rounded, granite hills,

or that, in seventy-five years' time,
one of her daughters will drive her
under this disappeared bridge
and out of Donegal
for the last time.
All she knows is that she is going to Ranafast
and that the train is travelling very slowly.

Halloween Windfalls

These mornings I gather the perfectly sweet apples,
which grew too high to pick,
which come down every night in the storm.

They crack and bruise easily
as they strike the grass.

Apples can't swivel on their twigs to catch the sun –
these are all half-red, half-green.

Blackbirds, tits, thrushes,
even crows have dug out their claims.

I wash off the dirt and the sticky leaves,
cut out the damaged bits,
set some sound, delicious ones aside.

I dry these and put some into a paper bag
to bring to my mother in the nursing home.

She used to set aside
the central leaves of the lettuce,
mash the heart of the cabbage
with a little butter and salt,
for the youngest.

Death,

the breath heavy and short –
a labour, mucky as birth.

My mother, at almost ninety,
must run a marathon.

Three weeks ago,
she made her last pithy retort;
three days ago, she ate a sliced strawberry;
today she cannot drink a sip –
we have pink sponges on sticks to wet her lips.

We, her greying brood, have arrived
in cars, by train, by plane.
Her room is full of stifled mobile phones.

Death's is a private country,
like love's.

The Red Tree

The red tree is a giver –
all day long it gives away its leaves,
one or two at a time.
When a dry leaf tumbles down through dry leaves
it sounds like the first drops of heavy rain.

In the evening
when all the last light comes to roost,
the red tree is a lamp
leading us into the dark.

Hedgehog

It snuffles across the lawn at night,
a small, silver, trundling boar
with a long nose.

We are seldom quiet enough
to allow the moon to find
with whom we share our ground.

RNA

for Harry Harvey

Last night, on Easter Sunday
my nephew told me
that messenger ribonucleic acids have the task
of translating DNA into protein,
that they carry a cell's blueprint
to be made into fibre and flesh and bone.

This morning I woke up early
but lay on.
My sister's garden was already wide awake.
Above all the chirping and whirring
the blackbird's courting note
rang out – a round gold coin.

Astonishing,
astonishing to know
that the throat muscles, the voice box
and the levitating architecture
of hollow feather and hollow bone,
were coded in the blackbird's DNA,
translated by messenger ribonucleic acids,
were made flesh,
this particular scrap of singing flesh,
which made this particular mating song.

Consider the Cocosphere

for Tim and Mairéad Robinson

Which you will never see
not because it lives in the ocean
but because it is so tiny
that light is too crude a medium
to relay to us
the absurdly beautiful structure
of the plate armour
which this alga creates for itself.

Paired porcelain cartwheels
interlock to form the sphere
which encloses this minute life form.
It drifts around,
just under the skin of the sea,
in blooms so large
they may be seen from space.

You will never see either the cocosphere
or the cocolithophore which it protects –
electrons are needed
to divine the form
of each individual design –
a beauty gratuitous,
as the upper, outer roofs
of cathedrals or mosques,
painstakingly decorated
for the eyes of steeplejacks
and of gods.

Blue Saxophones

In Buenos Aires the sidewalks are broken,
but the trees are tall and blue,
blue like Cezanne's blue pitcher,
which speaks to some still corner of the soul –
a quite unnecessary, delicate blue –
and the unmended pavements are strewn
with a carpet of blue blossoms,
and with the bent pennies,
the tough leathery purses,
which are the seed cases of the jacaranda –
a surety, until now,
that there would certainly
be more and more of this,
more tall blue trees in October,
singing, gratuitously,
above the dusty pavements
out of thousands of blue
clustered saxophones.

The Important Dead

for Sabine

In the long stone ship
of St Francis's Abbey
at Ross Errily,
in April evening light,
we decipher the names
of dead, defeated
chieftains, earls, burghers
whose bones were carried here
as Macbeth's were borne off to Iona
or other important dead were borne
to this great abbey or that.

Here, Kirwans, De Burgos, O Flahertys –
Old English, Mere Irish,
an occasional Cromwellian,
who lived in enmity,
amity or uneasy détente,
whose quarrels persist, vaguely,
only in our heads –
now rest, head to toe,
as the wind from the Black River
sifts over their sunken,
their stone-boxed, bones.

Near the bell tower,
our friend has been searching
for owl pellets – gluts of fur,
regurgitated by the soft-winged predators.
She dismantles them in her cupped hand.
As a gust scatters fragments of small skulls
she rescues the jawbone of a field mouse,
and the smaller jawbone of a bank vole,
a very recent invader.

In the Lava Pipe

None of the images of our fissured, creaking earth,
its armour-plating overlapping and melting
prepared me for life in the sloped tunnel
on a volcano's shoulder,
where a molten current once ran
under the cooling crust.

This is no longer a vision of red hell
but the land of shades itself.
This is life turned down
to its lowest register.
If we stand silent in the dark
we hear the soft wing beats of a bat;
if our ears were keener we might hear
the wing beats of the tiny insects
whose paths criss-cross in our torch-beams.

The curved walls are clothed in long roots.
They reach down for oxygen, a little moisture
and nutrients from bat-droppings.
Above us, certain flowering trees
grow along the route of the lava pipe,
their lives made possible
by this subterranean nourishment.

We reach the chamber at a rock fall
then turn our torch beams
and make our way back up,
hurrying as much as darkness,
broken rock and roots allow.
Rounding a curve, we see the bright oval
of the cave mouth,

This must be the path which Orpheus took,
his faith failing here, near the cave mouth,
his young beloved turning back
to the dank land of roots.

As he emerged weeping
the animals still understood his music
but, to his bright treble,
there was now added a deep bass
as he stumbled down the mountainside
following a line
of flowering trees.

The white cyclamen

has flung its five petals back
off its face and furled them
into a light-filled spiral.

It has done this because
it lives under a hazel
and needs to fight for light
and for the attention of bees
whose industry
in the service of sweetness
involves much casual sex
on the part of apple trees
and thistles and cyclamen.

We know that the dust
carried about on the thighs
of the world's bees
still sustains life
on our green and clamorous planet.
The mystery is why, despite
the imperatives of tooth and claw,
the tiny cyclamen's struggle
to propel itself out the soil
autumn after autumn,
millennium after millennium
should result in such grace.

Flowers at Loughcrew

How with this rage shall beauty hold a plea
Whose action is no stronger than a flower?
William Shakespeare, Sonnet 65

We have no key with which to enter
this chamber of the dead
so must peer through an iron gate
along the stone passage
to where a rising sun at equinox
will flash its torch
on flowers and suns –
a seeding and reaping calendar –
like suns and flowers
in a child's copybook.

A friend tells me
that fossil pollen is found
in the earliest burials.
He says this is what makes us human
as much as stone tools –
our ceremony of grief,
attended by what is most beautiful,
most fragrant on this earth.

Today is the last day of our winter.
Ice lingers under the stone lintel
but a brilliant sun reaches far
into the passage,
lights a corner of the backstone faintly,
gives us one carved flower,
picked out in white.

A family plays among the ruined cairns.
The father photographs them,
then gathers them to go
calling on the youngest,
to come along –
Bríd, Bríd.

Tomorrow is St Bridget's Day.
We drive home through soft pastureland.
In a low corner of a field
grow patches of greening rushes
and, near an old farmhouse,
on a slope,
strong clumps of snowdrops.

Apples and Fire

As we entered
the dark winter room
there, shining on the table
were apples, gathered
in haste last September –
each one a small lamp.

Later, as the stove's fire
carved into the cold
I began to understand
why fire was worshipped.

To share heat in winter
sweetness in winter,
is to know blessing.

Harmonic Vases

In the choir of the Collégiale Saint Martin,
just beneath the light-blasted gothic vaults,
are a number of small holes,
the openings of large ceramic pots
placed in the walls
to improve the acoustic.

Lucius Mummius, who destroyed
the theatre at Corinth,
transported its resonating
bronze vessels to Rome
and dedicated them
at the temple of Luna.

In cottages in County Clare,
an iron pot
was buried under the hearthstone
to give resonance to a dancer's step,
to contain the necessary emptiness

for though we wish to live
utterly alive, within our skins,
there lives in us another yearning –
that whatever harmonic is awakened in us
reverberate outwards,
through our voice, our step,
and outwards
and outwards.

He looks so carefully

at the fragrant honeysuckle
which I have gathered for him,
at the whirled, long, white and yellow petals,
at the long stamens,
which are grace itself
against that utter green.

He counts the furled and fretted blossoms;
notes how they are organised along the stem
in paired groups of two;
marvels at the mathematical regularity
of flowers –
that they should each be accorded
a precise number of petals,
that a code determining this
should be hidden
in something a millionth
of the size of a pinhead.

The doors
of perception
are multifarious.

Midday at Stockholm Airport

My flight delayed,
I wander into the Kapell beneath the escalator –
a dozen chairs, seats covered in light blue cloth,
a table,
beside it a small, red, unplugged wall-lamp
and an abstract tapestry –
sky, mountains, orange blobs which might be copper mines,
white lines in the foreground which might be cities.

Behind the door are a tiny sink
and a bookshelf. I read the titles –
Bibeln, Psalmboken, Siddur,
Koranens Budskap, Novum Testamentum Graece,
Agatha Christie's *Herkules Nya Storverk,*
below them red and blue prayer rugs, paper towels.

I light two candles
on a stylised Viking ship candelabra
although I know
that in some corner of the world,
men and women are being tortured
in the name of one or other
of the quiet books on the shelf,
I consider laying out the books on the table,
side by side in this peaceable city –

a man rushes in,
pulls out a mat,
pulls off his shoes,
washes his feet,
dries them with a paper towel
kneels down, his joints cracking,
touches the ground three times with his forehead,
repeats something three times,
rolls up the mat, puts on his shoes
and is gone.

All this was meant to be gone long ago,
votive lamps, lighting candles,
bowing towards some holy centre of the earth,
yet sometimes we have to
gather up the four corners of our lives,
like the corners of a tablecloth,
to shake out the crumbs;
sometimes we need light
for a journey,
sometimes we even need to bow.

Night Road in the Mountains

for the Berlin String Quintet

The great black hulks of the Bauges
rise so high
that, this midnight,
the plough's starry coulter
is sunk in them.

Earlier, in the small, crowded church,
in the upper valley,
five musicians played for us,
stood, bowed, then played on and on –
munificent as a mountain cascade in spring.

We do not know,
we do not understand
how five bows,
drawn across five sets of strings
by gifted, joyful hands, can trace
the back roads of our hearts,
which are rutted
with doubts and yearnings,
which are unpredictable
as this ever-swerving
mountain road
down which we now drive,
hugging the camber,

informed by rhythm
and cadence,
happy to live
between folded rock and stars.